STAR WARS
BE MORE LEIA

Written by Christian Blauvelt

Contents

Defining your goals 4
Choose your path 6
Understand the problem 8
Banish thoughts of failure 10
Don't wallow in self-pity 12
Ask for help if you need it 14

Taking the first steps 16
Suggest solutions 18
Be proactive 20
Stand up to bullies 22
Believe in yourself 24
Celebrate small victories 26

Forging your own path 28
Lead by example 30
Get your priorities straight 32
Don't worry what others think 34
Trust your instincts 36
Don't quit when things get tough 38

Building a community 40
Unify your allies 42
Prove your loyalty 44
Lean on your community 46
Purge outdated ideas 48
Take it to the next level 50

Leading with confidence 52
Be the boss 54
Own your success 56
Your time is precious 58
Don't suffer fools 60
Keep pushing 62

Introduction

The rebel's path to positive change

Does it ever seem like a tough situation won't get better? Don't let doubt or fear hold you back. If something needs to change—an injustice needs to be overturned, a wrong needs to be righted, an Empire needs to be toppled—you are the one who can step up and make it happen. Your path won't be a straight and easy one: not everyone will agree with you and setbacks are inevitable. But don't get carbonite-cold feet. You are the spark that will light the fire that will make true transformation possible.

Be More Leia provides heartening guidance on how to take action and effect positive change. You will be empowered by the brave insights of a legendary princess and rebel leader—and you won't even need to brave the cold of Hoth.

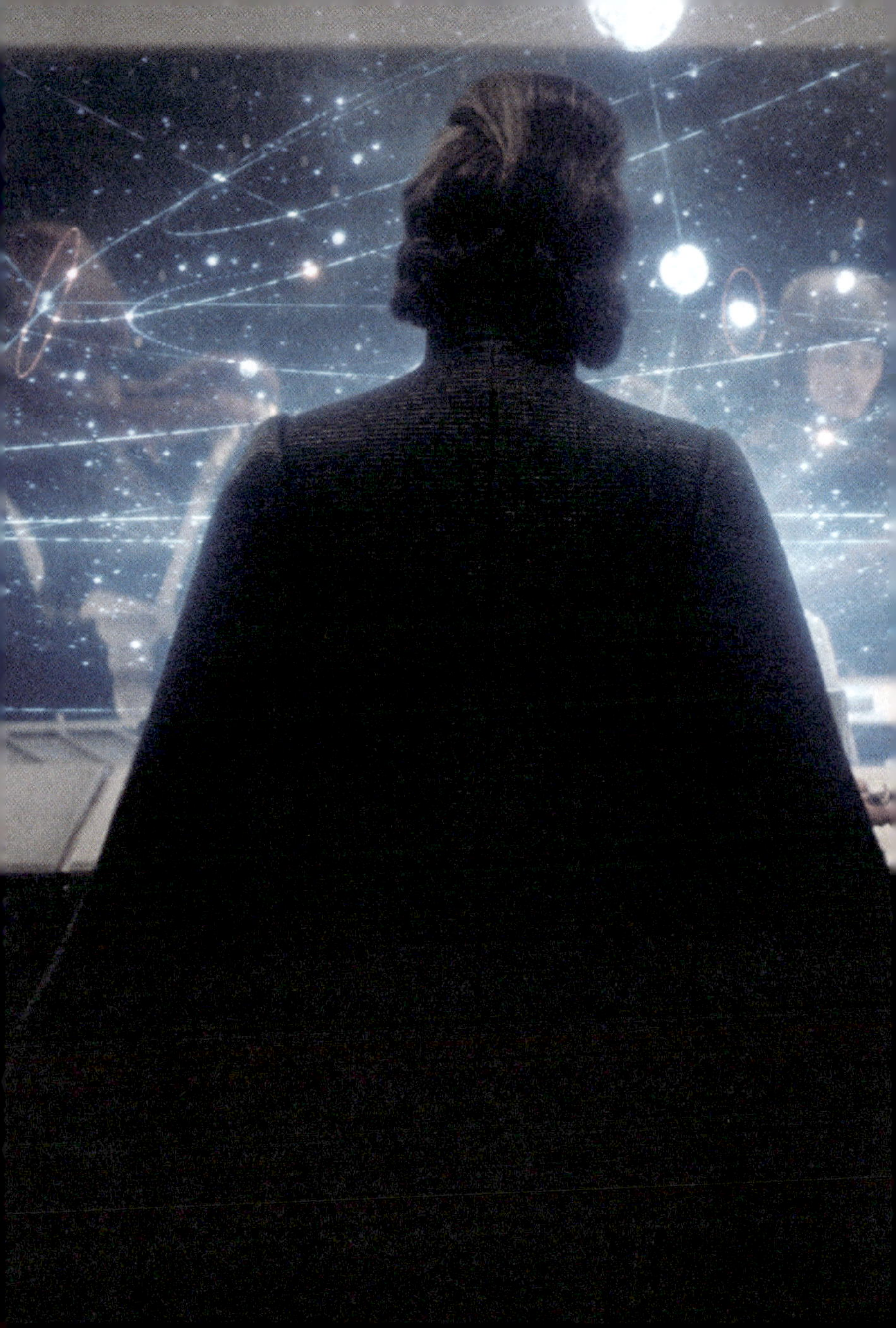

DEFINING YOUR GOALS

Every journey has a beginning. Whether you're raising money for a good cause, hoping to change public opinion, or battling galactic tyranny, figuring out where you're starting and what you want to achieve is essential. Create clear, targeted objectives to ensure you hit the mark ... or maybe even a small thermal exhaust port.

"He's got to follow his own path.
No one can choose it for him."
Princess Leia

Defining your goals

Choose your path

If something is wrong—a friend has suffered an insult for being different, your boss refuses to listen to any ideas but their own, a masked warlord has blasted your home planet into atoms—you have a choice: do nothing, or try and make a difference. The road to change is not easy. No one can force you to be a rebel; you alone must decide to fight for what's right.

"Get your head out of your cockpit. There are things you cannot solve."
General Organa

Defining your goals

Understand the problem

Study the situation before you rush off to face it.
Come up with a plan, get the training you need, and
listen to the advice of others, because there are some
problems you can't vaporize in your X-wing alone.
Being short-sighted about how to raise a complaint
with company leadership or how to execute that
funding drive can be just as foolish as wasting all
your fuel to flee an enemy that's just going to
follow you anyway.

"Never tell me the odds."
Han Solo

Defining your goals

Banish thoughts of failure

You'll never win supporters for your cause if you doubt yourself. Identify your skill set and be confident about it: worry won't get you past that Imperial blockade or effect any meaningful change. Having confidence doesn't mean being cocky, though: double check that the cave where you've landed isn't the belly of a giant space worm or, worse, that you're not about to hit "reply all" to that email.

"We have no time for sorrows, Commander."
Princess Leia

Don't wallow in self-pity

Attitude is everything when you're working to achieve a big goal, and regrets only direct your attention to the past, not the present where it belongs. Turn that pain into action. It can mean channeling your feelings into humor—a gag about a trooper falling short of the Imperial Stormtrooper Corps' height requirements is always good—or briefing your team on your battle strategy to make sure the wrong you're trying to right never happens again. Planning tops pouting.

"Help me, Obi-Wan Kenobi.
You're my only hope."
Princess Leia

Defining your goals

Ask for help if you need it

No rebel ever brought down a whole Empire by herself: any big change you're fighting for requires the time, skills, and advice of many. You'll need contributors to raise money for a deserving teen's college tuition, volunteers to clean up your local park, maybe an aging hermit to escort your R2 unit past watchful Imperial eyes. A team is always a stronger force for change than someone fighting solo.

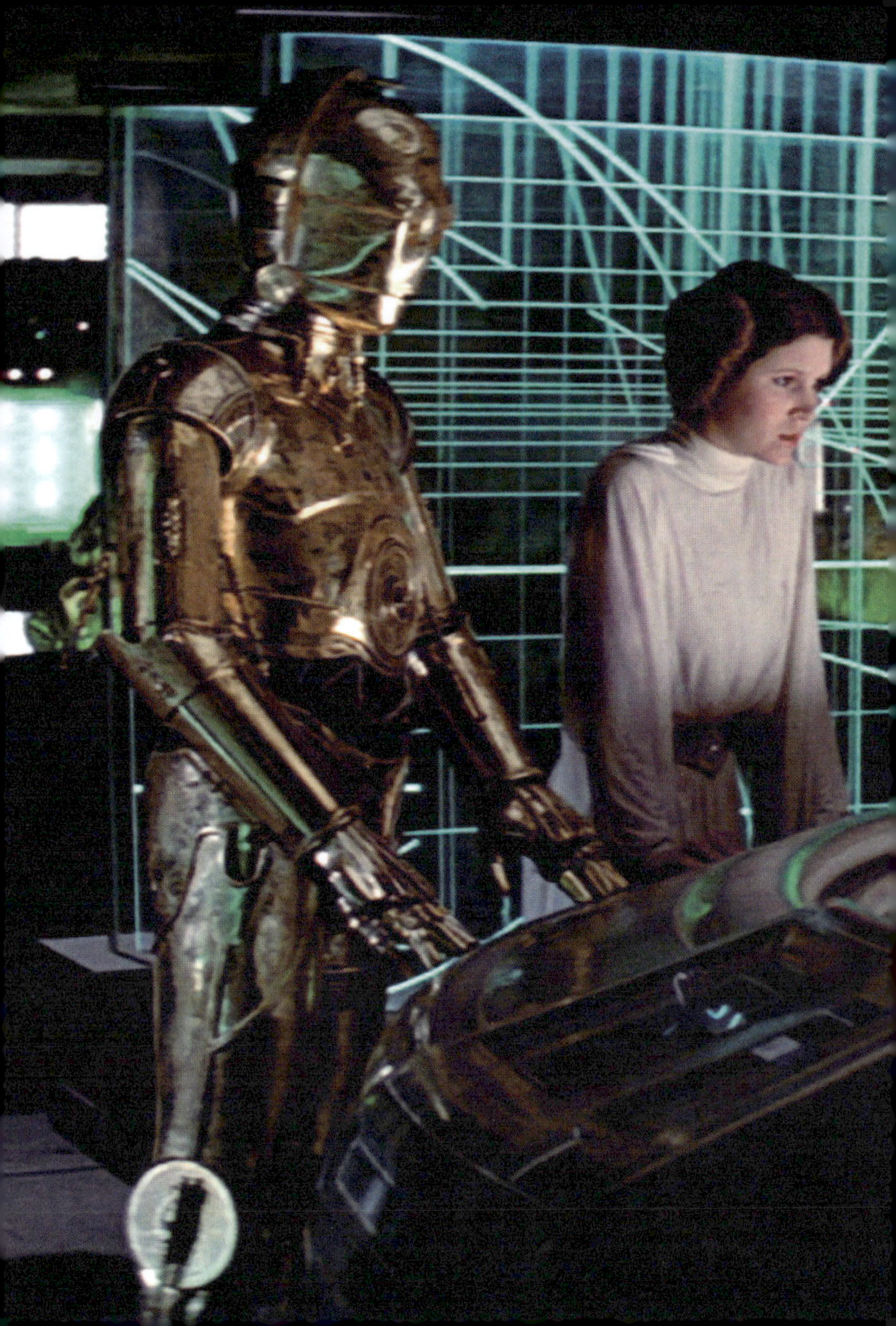

TAKING THE FIRST STEPS

You know what you want to change and what success will look like once you've achieved your goals. But knowing how to deactivate the tractor beam keeping you on board a Death Star isn't enough: you must take action to get real results. Roll up the sleeves of your senator's robes, and get to work.

"Somebody has to save our skins. Into the garbage chute, flyboy."
Princess Leia

Taking the first steps

Suggest solutions

Put your brain to use, not just your blaster.
A tough problem might be in front of you: how do
you amplify your message, get that hashtag trending,
or find your way out of an Imperial prison block?
Thinking outside the box, then communicating your
problem-solving idea to your team quickly, clearly,
and forcefully will motivate them and get results.
Keep improvising, though, in case your brilliant idea
sends you out of a dungeon and into a dianoga den.

"This is something
I must do myself."
Padmé Amidala

Taking the first steps

Be proactive

Having a vision is not enough: you need to take action if you want to make a difference. You can have the best plan ever mapped out on your blackboard, laptop, or holoprojector, but without being willing to fire a grappling gun and ascend to your target destination yourself, you can't really expect anyone else on your team to do so. And you certainly can't afford to be beholden to the timetable of others—not even that of the Galactic Senate. Take the first step, and others will follow.

"If you strike me down, I shall become more powerful than you can possibly imagine."
Obi-Wan Kenobi

Taking the first steps

Stand up to bullies

Foes will try to derail your mission. They will attempt to diminish you, discredit you, or destroy you with a lightsaber. Hold your ground. Let them know you are not afraid. And if your opponents continue with their bullying agenda, tell them they are only revealing their own weakness and insecurity. They have demonstrated fear, anger, and hate. And we all know where that leads.

"I am a Jedi, like my father before me."
Luke Skywalker

Taking the first steps

Believe in yourself

Believe you're doing the right thing, no matter how much others try to rattle you. Some may say that you're making the fight all about you or that you're no different to the bullies you're standing up to. A healthy dose of introspection never hurts, but don't let others get in your head. If some hood-wearing fiend says you're full of hate, prove him wrong with your courage and compassion. No one who shoots lightning from their fingertips should define you.

"You've taken your first step into a larger world."
Obi-Wan Kenobi

Celebrate small victories

Acknowledging success, no matter how incremental, is essential. Maybe you're recognizing a follower milestone, or a fundraising goal, or you just connected with the Force for the first time despite being about 15 years older than most first-time Force users. Giving, and graciously receiving, a well-deserved pat on the back can be as meaningful as a medal ceremony, and it puts you and your team in the right frame of mind to achieve further goals. It's the positive reinforcement you're looking for.

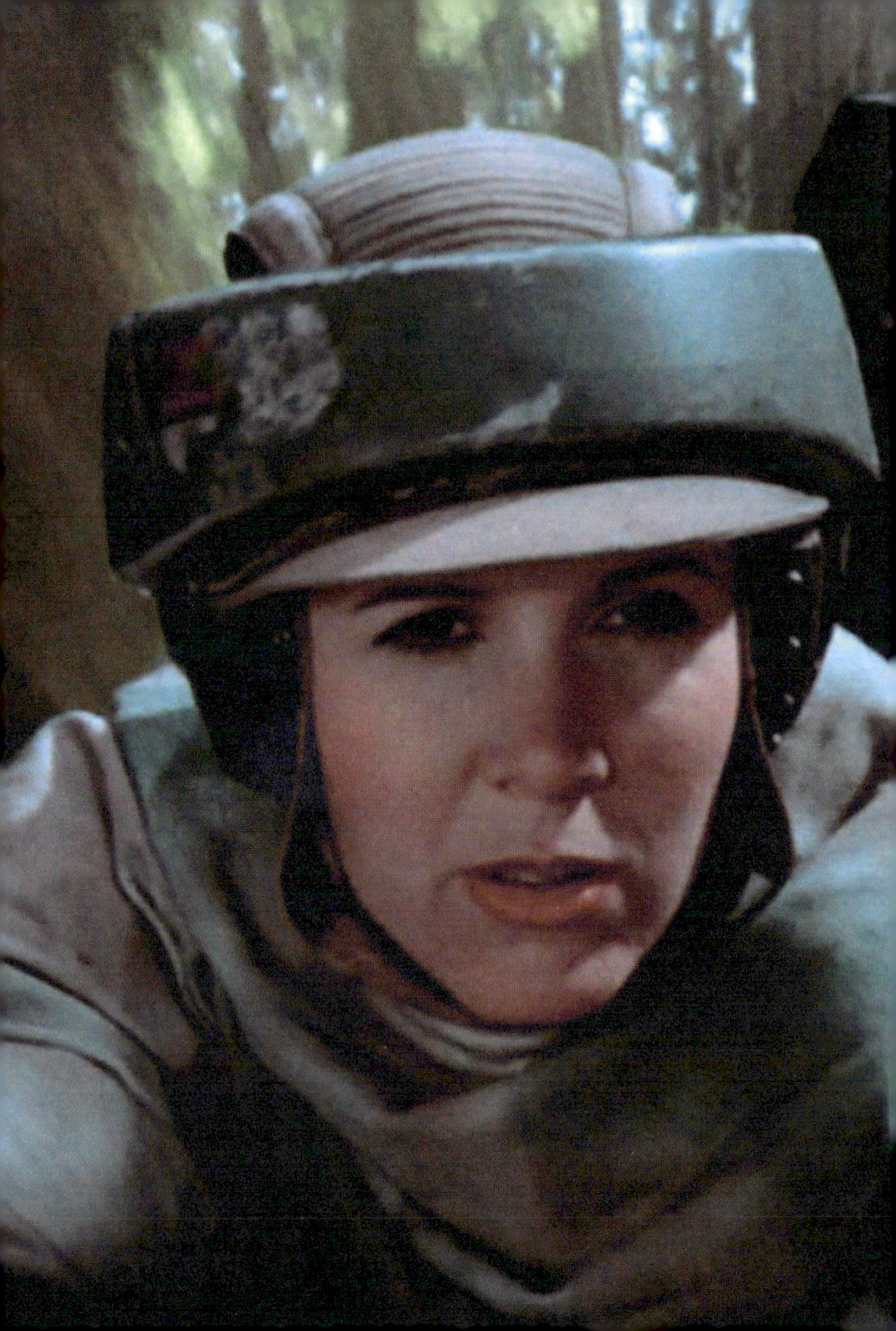

FORGING YOUR OWN PATH

Getting started can be the hardest part of a journey, but building on your initial achievements can seem almost as daunting: you may have taken down a Death Star, but you still have an entire Empire to defeat. This is uncharted territory and it is up to you to navigate it. Keep calm, stay focused, and watch out for unexpected Ewok traps.

"Would it help if I got out and pushed?"
Princess Leia

Forging your own path

Lead by example

You're not going to overthrow a galactic tyrant if you expect hard work from everyone but yourself. A great leader not only inspires action, she initiates it. Show up on time, put in the hours, get your hands dirty, even draw blaster fire if you must—it'll show those fighting alongside you that you're not just a leader, you're one of them. Even a sarcastic joke can be enough to give your followers the kick they need. And if all else fails, stick to your guns ... and get out and push!

"She was more interested in protecting the light than seeming like a hero."
General Organa about Vice Admiral Holdo

Forging your own path

Get your priorities straight

The campaign is not about you. It is bigger than any individual, no matter who they are: Jedi or Jawa. It is about righting wrongs, fighting for justice, saving a fleet of rebels who all face the same persecutions as you. Your mind-set must be goal-oriented. Leave personal glory for celebrities, bounty hunters, and Supreme Chancellors—and remember that YOU are making a real difference.

"Size matters not. Look at me. Judge me by my size, do you? And well you should not."
Yoda

Don't worry what others think

True power comes from within. Whether you have a burning desire for change, the unshakable belief that you are following the path of justice, or a midi-chlorian count so high it is off the charts, nobody can take that away from you. The best way to silence doubters is to prove them wrong. So, if you know that you can lift a starship out of a swamp using only your mind, who's to stop you?

"I know how to run without you holding my hand!"
Rey

Forging your own path

Trust your instincts

Embarking on a quest is often an invitation for others to offer their opinions. Some advice can provide useful context to your situation, like learning that your new droid friend is wanted by the galaxy's most dastardly villains. Unwanted advice, however, can be as unwelcome as a happabore's snout in your drinking water. Be confident enough to trust your instincts—especially when you have the home-planet advantage—and learn how to refuse advice firmly, but politely.

"Hope is like the sun. If you only believe in it when you see it, you'll never make it through the night."

Vice Admiral Holdo, quoting General Organa

Don't quit when things get tough

When fighting for a cause, things won't always go your way. At times it will seem dark. Very dark. You may face colleagues who don't trust you to act in their best interest. You will face scorn from strangers and friends alike. Sometimes it will feel as though you are the only one who can see the big picture. But know that darkness can't last forever—you will find your way through it, even if it feels like you're the sole passenger in an enormous star cruiser in the vacuum of space.

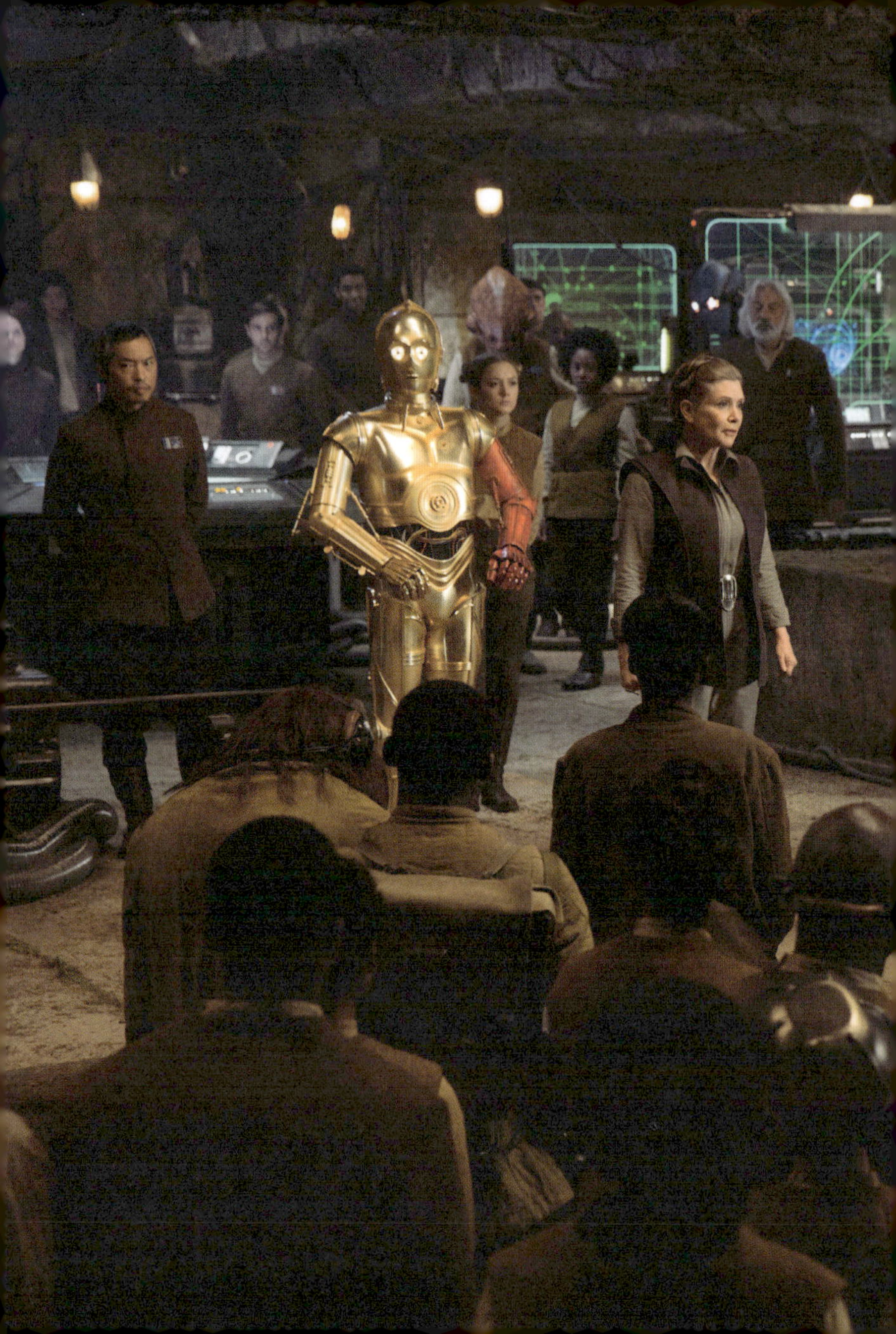

BUILDING A COMMUNITY

A rebellion of one is unlikely to be particularly effective. True change only comes through sustained, collective effort. How you build a community—by inspiring other rebels, leading with conviction, and repeatedly relocating to secure, secret bases—will determine if you truly have a new hope.

"Rebellions are built on hope."
Jyn Erso

Building a community

Unify your allies

Seek out people who share your beliefs and help provide a little direction to channel their energies toward a singular goal. They might be great at making phone calls, a star at crafting social media strategy, or startlingly capable of taking out a squad of stormtroopers blind with nothing but a big stick. Once roles are defined, rally your people to achieve a critical objective: those Death Star plans aren't going to steal themselves.

"My fate will be no different from that of our people."
Padmé Amidala

Building a community

Prove your loyalty

Internet trolls getting you down? Rival companies poaching your top employees? Droid army invading your planet? Show that you're a true believer when times are tough. Stand front and center with your allies to ensure they won't waver. If you show you're willing to take hostile fire, whether toxic tweets or battleship blasts, you'll inspire your community by the risks you've taken on their behalf, and strengthen their resolve to march on.

"We have powerful friends.
You're gonna regret this…"
Princess Leia

Lean on your community

Inspiring others is a tough, and sometimes lonely, role. But you should rely on your allies as well. Whether that means calling in reinforcements to gather a crowd, or shamelessly name-dropping during a meeting, it never hurts to give a sense of your collective muscle. Be realistic about how quickly your community can rally, though, or you may find yourself chained to a bad-tempered slug crime lord for a while before your support arrives.

"You must unlearn what you have learned."
Yoda

Purge outdated ideas

The masses are resistant to change, but it is time to shake up the status quo and usher in new ideas. Society might be governed by outdated rules, Senates might be ruled by Sith Lords disguised as politicians, and ordinary people might not believe that a tiny green creature can be all-powerful with the Force. But times are changing. Be the first to say, "I have a good feeling about this."

"Now, be brave and don't look back. Don't look back."

Shmi Skywalker

Building a community

Take it to the next level

You've achieved your initial goals: you earned the recognition you were looking for, grew the size of your movement, won the Boonta Eve Classic in exhilarating fashion, and had all the naysayers saying "poodoo!" Now what? It's time to think about new, even bigger goals. Can you reach a new audience on a different platform? Become part of an even bigger conversation? Expand your organization? It's time to roll the chance cube again, even if it means you reach a point of no return.

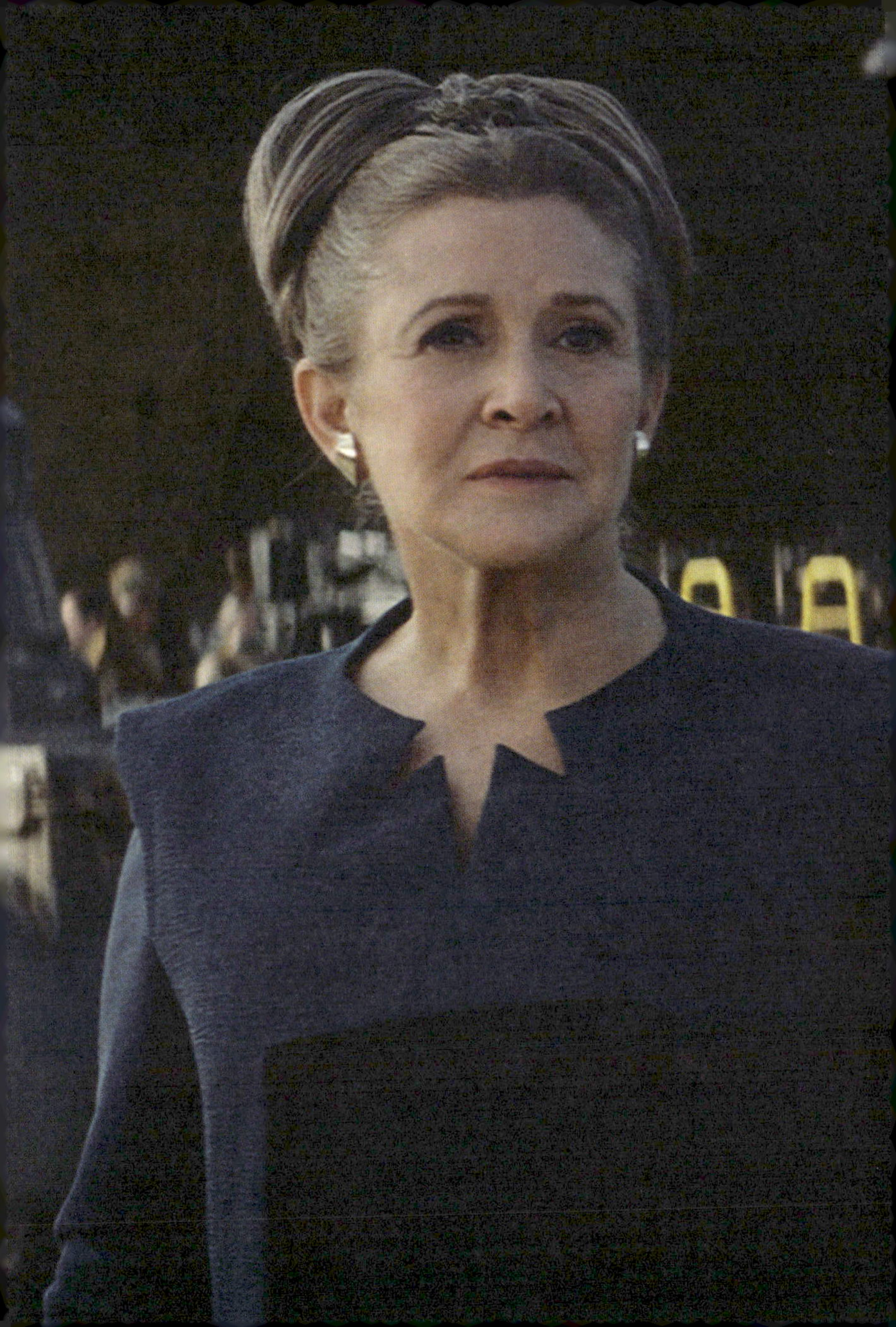

LEADING WITH CONFIDENCE

Having allies is essential, but you need to know how to focus their efforts, especially if your Rebel Alliance is fast becoming a New Republic. You have to lead. First you must clarify your priorities: what do you need to handle, what can you delegate? Next, you must perfect your leadership style—will it be Princess, General, or somewhere in between?

"I don't know who you are, or where you came from, but from now on, you do as I tell you, okay?"
Princess Leia

Leading with confidence

Be the boss

Remember who got you here: you! A leader needs to be confident telling people what to do. If there's pushback, make it clear that your directions are not suggestions but orders. Whether you are speaking to a new contact, an old employee, or a complete stranger who thinks he is rescuing you from a Death Star prison, make sure you assert your authority quickly and forcefully. Clear with your HR team first that the phrases "scruffy looking" and "nerf herder" are acceptable feedback.

"In my experience, there is no such thing as luck."

Obi-Wan Kenobi

Leading with confidence

Own your success

You've worked hard, and you should own it. Don't let others write off your successes as pure luck; it diminishes your achievements and belittles you. Make sure you declare the value of what you've done: putting in those late hours at the office, crafting a rousing message that has attracted intergalactic support, deflecting blaster bolts blindfolded. This adds value to your cause and gives credence to you as leader.

"Will somebody get this big walking carpet out of my way?"
Princess Leia

Your time is precious

You need to be decisive: no 20-part email threads debating the best way to proceed. Choose what to do and end the discussion. You've got partnerships to negotiate, meetings to lead, budgets to balance, and galactic regimes to topple. So don't let busywork that can be handled by a few choice droids drag you under like dianoga fodder. Good time management skills can be the difference between escaping through that trash compactor and being crushed by it.

"I don't know where you get your delusions, laser brain."
Princess Leia

Leading with confidence

Don't suffer fools

Fighting for your cause can take its toll, especially if you're holed up in an underground base on a remote ice planet. There's no reason your campaign hub can't have a relaxed atmosphere, but there is always someone who takes the joke too far. Keep an eye on the troublemakers and set them straight right away.
Let it be known that you will go to the ends of the Outer Rim to rescue your teammates from blocks of frozen carbonite ... but inappropriate workplace frivolity will not be tolerated.

"It's now or never."
General Organa

Keep pushing

Just because you've achieved your initial goal doesn't mean you should stop. If you don't act now, then when? Keep targeting Death Stars of oppression; keep defying the Snokes and Palpatines of your world; keep swinging across the chasms of social injustice. Rebel, resist, lead, inspire—and never cease—to ensure the dark side is always kept at bay.

Penguin Random House

Project Editor Shari Last
Project Art Editor Jon Hall
Pre-production Producer Siu Yin Chan
Senior Producer Mary Slater
Managing Editor Sadie Smith
Managing Art Editor Vicky Short
Publisher Julie Ferris
Art Director Lisa Lanzarini
Publishing Director Simon Beecroft

DK would like to thank: Sammy Holland, Michael Siglain, Jennifer Heddle, Troy Alders, Leland Chee, Matt Martin, Pablo Hidalgo, Nicole LaCoursiere, Bryce Pinkos, Erik Sanchez, and Kelly Jensen at Lucasfilm; Chelsea Alon at Disney Publishing; and Megan Douglass for proofreading.

First American Edition, 2019
Published in the United States by DK Publishing
1450 Broadway, Suite 801, New York, NY 10018

Copyright © 2019 Dorling Kindersley Limited
DK, a Division of Penguin Random House LLC
20 21 22 23 10 9 8 7 6 5 4 3 2 1
001-317165-Mar/2020

© & TM 2019 LUCASFILM LTD.

All rights reserved. Without limiting the rights under the copyright reserved above, no part of this publication may be reproduced, stored in or introduced into a retrieval system, or transmitted, in any form, or by any means (electronic, mechanical, photocopying, recording, or otherwise), without the prior written permission of the copyright owner.
Published in Great Britain by Dorling Kindersley Limited.

A catalog record for this book is available from the Library of Congress.

ISBN: 978-1-4654-7897-9

DK books are available at special discounts when purchased in bulk for sales promotions, premiums, fund-raising, or educational use. For details, contact: DK Publishing Special Markets, 1450 Broadway, Suite 801, New York, NY 10018. SpecialSales@dk.com

Printed and bound in China

A WORLD OF IDEAS:
SEE ALL THERE IS TO KNOW

www.dk.com
www.starwars.com